God's Design for Christian Dating

GREG LAURIE

HARVEST HOUSE PUBLISHERS
Eugene, Oregon 97405

GOD'S DESIGN FOR CHRISTIAN DATING

Copyright © 1983 by Harvest House Publishers
Eugene, Oregon 97402

Library of Congress Catalog Card Number 82-083836
ISBN 0-89081-373-6

Printed in the United States of America.

PREFACE

Singles are one of the fastest-growing groups in the United States. Between 1970 and 1982, the number of people living alone swelled from 10.9 million to 19.4 million. That's a 78 percent jump. unprecedented in U.S. history!

In addition to those who are living alone are those who are living with their parents. Many of these are wondering about that person they will meet one day with whom they will perhaps spend the rest of their lives. There's another group of singles—those who have suffered through divorce. That number has soared also. From 1970 to 1981 the number of divorced people living by themselves grew from 1.5 million to 3.7 million, an increase of 150 percent!

There is so much uncertainty as a single; much of life is geared to the family. The American dream is a family living together in a house with a white picket fence and a rose garden. Many single people are confused and wondering if there is any purpose or direction for their lives. They are attempting to find that perfect mate through things like computer dating services, singles bars, and singles retreats. Some people have even put advertisements in local and national magazines telling about the qualities they are looking for in a husband or a wife.

Yet there is a change taking place in the singles scene. According to one expert, people have tried sexual freedom and have found that it wasn't so great. So they have swung around to more traditional values. Many singles are looking for absolutes; they are tired of the loose lifestyle and want a person they can commit themselves to.

This book is for that kind of person—the one who wants absolutes, who wants to know that there is an order, a purpose, and a plan for the single person. I hope you will read this book with an open mind, because I believe that God has a plan for you. God created you with a need for another individual. He wants to fill that loneliness in your life. I pray that you will let Him reveal His plan to you.

—Greg Laurie

CONTENTS

God's Design for Christian Dating

1

The Starting Point

I assume that I am writing to a variety of people. Many of you are young and have never been married. Some of you may be divorced. Some may be single parents. Others are widows. God may have called a few of you to a life of singleness or celibacy. Whatever your situation, God is concerned about your need.

Probably most of you are asking the question, "Who does God want me to marry?" I believe God has a partner picked out for you. If you desire to marry, you should not feel guilty about it or try to suppress it. But I believe we need to look at that desire in light of the Word of God.

Each of you will look at dating from a slightly different perspective. I would like to show you what God has to say about the subject. If you look in a Bible concordance under "D" for dating, you won't find any references to the subject. But you will find a lot of principles in Scripture that relate directly to relationships between men and women. So we will actually talk very little about the specific details of dating, but concentrate instead on the principles that ultimately determine the success or failure of any dating or marriage relationship.

God's Perspective

Today it is more important than ever to examine God's perspective in dating because Hollywood and Madison Avenue have sold us a bad bill of goods. They have told us that when we meet that perfect guy or that perfect girl, violins will swell in the background as we see each other on the beach and run (in slow motion, of course) into each other's arms, fall in love, and live together happily ever after.

We only have to look at an ever-increasing divorce rate to know that this is not true. Experts say that between one-out-of-two and one-out-of-three marriages ends in divorce. The number of divorces has more than tripled in the last 20 years. One person has said, "Marriage is a three-ring circus—engagement ring, wedding ring, and suffering." That's how it is for a lot of people, because they start out with a false concept of marriage. Most singles look for that perfect person who will fill the void in their lives. Through marriage, they expect the end of all their loneliness, that they will never be sad again, that their sexual desires will be fulfilled, and that all their sexual temptations will disappear.

The cliche, "The grass is greener on the other side," expresses what many people think. I hear married people say, "I remember the good old days when I was single. I could go anywhere and do anything I wanted. Now I'm married and I'm stuck with a wife and kids to support." Singles envy those who are married, and married people envy singles. The fact is that there are advantages and disadvantages to both.

The Bible teaches us to be content where we are right now. The Apostle Paul wrote, "I have learned, in whatever state I am, therewith to be content."[1] Are you content as a single? Or are you thinking that when you get married, then you will be really happy? You might consider the advantages of being unattached. Paul wrote in 1 Corinthians 7, "My desire is to have you free from all anxiety.... The unmarried [man] is anxious about the things of the Lord, how he may please the Lord; but the married man is anxious about wordly matters, how he may please his wife.... And the unmarried woman or girl is concerned and anxious about the matters of the Lord, how to be wholly separated and set apart in body and spirit; but the married woman has her cares [centered] in earthly affairs, how she may please her husband."[2]

Finding God's Calling

I am very happily married. I have a wife and a son who was born a year after we were married. When I got married—Cathe was 18 and I was 21—it was a difficult adjustment for me. For the first few years of our marriage I had a "single mentality." I would do what I wanted to do and spend money where I wanted to spend it. It took me a while to realize that I had responsibilities first to my family, and that God held me accountable for them. I didn't have the mobility and freedom I once had.

In one sense I envy you singles. Most of you have the ability to pack your bags and move at the snap of a heavenly finger. I can't do that very easily. It would be a major production for me or anyone who is married and has children. But as a single person you can respond more quickly to what God calls you to do. God might call you to another country, and if you are willing and open to the Holy Spirit, you could go because you have the freedom and mobility to do so.

Paul also says this in 1 Corinthians 7: "Art thou bound to a wife? Seek not to be loosed. Art thou loosed from a wife? Seek not a wife."[3] Paul tells singles, "Don't seek a wife." That's hard to do. Before I was married, I was seeking a wife. In fact, it seemed like every girl I'd meet, I'd think, "Is this the one, Lord?" I wanted to be married more than anything else. The problem is that this attitude can easily mislead us. We can be drawn to someone by a physical attraction and miss the person God has chosen for us.

So what's the alternative? **The important issue is not to *find* the right person, but to *be* the right person.** In Romans 12:1 Paul says, "I beseech you, therefore, brethren, by the mercies of God, that ye present your bodies a living sacrifice, holy, acceptable unto God, which is your reasonable service." The word "beseech" could be translated "strongly urge." Paul is strongly urging us to present ourselves to God as living sacrifices. The problem with living sacrifices is that they tend to squirm off the altar. Most living sacrifices don't want to be sacrifices.

God is saying that you must first present yourself to Him. This is not something you do once in your life. This is something you do on a daily basis, sometimes even on an hourly basis. You are constantly presenting yourself to the Lord, saying, "Lord here I am. I offer myself to You. I want Your will in my life."

Then Paul writes, "Be not conformed to this world, but be transformed by the renewing of your mind, that ye may prove what is that good and acceptable and perfect will of God."[4]

We live in a world that is saturated with sex. Our TV sitcoms are filled with sexually suggestive remarks. Magazines display models in suggestive dress, too. As a result, many people find themselves constantly thinking about sex. It is built up to be the ultimate of experiences. Paul says that this emphasis is in the wrong area. He tells us, "Don't be conformed to this world."

If you're a child of God, you must not listen to the garbage the world is feeding you. It isn't working. Let's get back to God's plan and realize that sex is something God created. It's wonderful and pleasurable and good in its proper place, but it is only a minor part of life. The Word of God needs to give our minds a good thorough washing. The reason is that we may know what is the *good* and *acceptable* and *perfect* will of God. God has a perfect plan for your life. Don't settle for second best!

First the Kingdom

When I was caught in my "have-to-be-married" syndrome, I was always praying "Lord, send me a wife. I need a wife." I was constantly looking for the woman who would be my wife. Finally the Lord brought my attention to Matthew 6:33, which says, "Seek ye first the kingdom of God and His righteouness, and all these things shall be added unto you."

I read that and thought, "Aha! I've found the secret." So I started going to the Lord and saying, "Lord, I'm seeking You. Now where is she?" The Lord showed me that I wasn't truly seeking Him; I was seeking a wife. I thought, "I'm down on my knees praying." But the Lord showed me that the only reason I was in prayer was to find a wife. He said, "You need to seek *Me*."

What does it mean to seek first the kingdom of God? It means to let Jesus Christ be Lord of every aspect of your life, including your singleness. We are also told to seek "His righteousness," which means living a life that is pleasing to God. If I seek first His kingdom and His righteousness, He will add all the other things I need.

Then the Lord showed me Psalm 37:4, which says, "Delight thyself also in the Lord, and He shall give thee the desires of thine heart." Again

I got caught in the trap of "delighting myself in the Lord" simply to gain the desire of my heart, which was of course a girl. The Lord brought me back to what the Scripture says: I was not to delight myself in a *girl*, but in the *Lord*.

What does it mean to "delight"? It means "to gladden or take joy in." That verse says to take joy in nothing else but the Lord Jesus Christ. It doesn't mean to delight in Jesus *if* He gives you what you want. When God gives you the desires of your heart, those are fringe benefits. But I can't seek for those things; I must seek only to please God, to know Him, to discover His kingdom in my life, to find His righteousness, to delight in Him.

When you delight yourself in the Lord, your desires are going to start changing. The passion and pursuit of your life is not going to be simply to find a guy or a girl. That can even diminish completely.

When I started truly seeking the Lord and delighting in Him, my thoughts were no longer always on girls. When I was in church and I saw an attractive girl, I wasn't thinking, "Is that her?" All I cared about was what God wanted. After awhile it honestly didn't matter anymore.

So the main lesson I learned was that God wasn't so concerned with *who I married* as with *who I was.* But how then does one know who he or she is to marry? For that we need to look at some more Scriptures.

1. Philippians 4:11.
2. 1 Corinthians 7:32-34 (AMP).
3. 1 Corinthians 7:27.
4. Romans 12:2.

2

God's Timing, Your Patience

Do you realize that God is concerned about *every* aspect of your life? Jesus told His disciples, "Are not two sparrows sold for a farthing? And one of them shall not fall on the ground without your Father. But the very hairs of your head are all numbered. Fear ye not therefore, ye are of more value than many sparrows."[1] If God is concerned about such a small detail as the number of hairs on your head, how much more is He concerned about the man or woman with whom you will spend the rest of your life?

Isaac and Rebekah

One of the best love stories in the Bible is the story about Isaac and his wife, Rebekah. In the ancient Hebrew culture, a man didn't choose his own wife, but his father chose her for him. Isaac's father, Abraham, did not want his son to marry one of the Canaanite women in that region, so he asked his most trusted servant to go to relatives in Mesopotamia and find a bride for Isaac.

The servant took ten camels on the trip and went to the city of Nahor. There, in the late afternoon, he and his camels waited by the city well, and he prayed a prayer something like this: "Lord, I don't know who the girl is that You have picked out for my master, Isaac. But as I wait by this well while the women of the city come to draw water, I pray that the one You have called to marry Isaac, when I ask her for a drink of water, will not only offer me water, but my camels also."

As soon as he finished that prayer, he saw a beautiful young girl whose name was Rebekah, a daughter of Abraham's brother. When he asked her for a drink of water, she gave him all he wanted, and then said she would draw water for his camels also. Now that's a big job. After a long trip through the desert, each camel would drink about 20 gallons. For ten camels that was probably an hour's worth of work. But she did it, even as the servant had prayed she would.

After thanking God for this answer to prayer, the servant met Rebekah's family and told them his story. Then he asked them if they would allow Rebekah to go and marry Isaac. When they agreed, he gave them silver and gold, clothing, and other valuable items.

After the servant spent the night, he was eager to return home. But Laban, Rebekah's brother said, "Let her stay a few days." The servant said, "No, don't hold me back, seeing as how God has prospered my way." So they asked Rebekah, and when she agreed to go, they got on the camels and rode back to Israel.

What is so thought-provoking about this story is that while all of this was transpiring, Isaac wasn't running around saying, "God, where is she? Is she over here? Is she over there?" It just says that in the evening Isaac was in the fields meditating. He was seeking first the kingdom of God. He was looking to the Lord. One night, as he looked on the horizon, he saw the silhouette of the camels, and as they got closer he saw Rebekah, the beautiful maiden whom the Lord was bringing to him. It says that Isaac took Rebekah, and she became his wife, and he loved her.

What It Means for Me

There are some interesting parallels in this story with what God wants us to experience today. First, the father chose the wife in that culture. In that same way, your heavenly Father wants to choose whom you are to marry. Now you may have some plans. I sometimes ask single girls, "What kind of guy would you like to marry?" I've heard them respond, "Well, he has to be six feet tall, good-looking, with dark hair, and drive a Porsche." Sometimes it's interesting to see them when they fall in love. The guy can be four-feet-one, have no hair at all, be overweight, and ride a moped!

The fact is that God has chosen a certain person for you, because He knows you best, and He knows that other person, and He's changing both of you every day.

One day you're going to meet that special person, and you will be prepared for each other. You will be just what that other person needs, and he will be just what you need.

The second parallel is God's timing. Isaac was probably in his late thirties when he married. But he was seeking the Lord rather than tearing up the landscape looking for a wife. Does that mean you should never be around girls or guys? Not at all. Get out there! Look around! There's nothing wrong with that. But don't be obsessed with it. Don't go running around making that the passion and pursuit of your life. The Lord will show you the right person at the right time. In the meantime, while you are waiting, the best thing you can do is to seek Him.

By nature I am an impatient person. I do not like to wait for anything. If I see a line in a store, I will go out of my way to avoid it. So when God said to be patient and wait for Him to bring that girl, it was hard for me to do. It wasn't too long after I started seeking only the Lord that He brought Cathe into my life. It wasn't love at first sight. We just met and started getting to know each other. We actually had broken up when God spoke to my heart and said I was to marry Cathe. It turned out that at almost the same hour God had spoken to her about me!

Once I learned that Cathe was to be my wife, I wanted to rush right into marriage. But God responded, "No, along with my calling I have my timing. You must learn to wait upon me." One of the attributes of God's love is found in 1 Corinthians 13:4, which says, "Love is patient."

For the most part, we don't have long courtships anymore. Often couples come to the church where I pastor for marriage counseling. They come up to me and ask if I'll perform the ceremony. I ask them, "How long have you known each other?"

"A month," they say.

"When do you want to get married?"

"Next week."

"What's the big rush?" I ask them. Usually the answer is, "We're in love." Normally I suggest that they wait and get to know each other a little better. I find that often the real reason a couple wants to get married so quickly is that they want to hop in the sack. They can't control their sexual desires, and rather than live in adultery, they decide that marriage is the answer. But God's love is patient. Sex is not a suitable foundation for building a relationship.

Jacob and Rachel

The Book of Genesis has a good story about patience in a man named Jacob. He fell in love with a girl named Rachel. Jacob was a pretty forceful guy, and when he saw Rachel for the first time and noticed her beauty, he went up and kissed her. Then it says he lifted up his voice and wept. I don't know if Rachel was a bad kisser or what. But I think he wept because he knew that this was the girl the Lord had brought to him.

Jacob went right to Rachel's father, Laban, and said he wanted to marry her. They talked and determined that Jacob would work seven years for Laban before he could marry Rachel. You know what most guys would have done? They would have said, "See you later. There are other fish in the ocean." But not Jacob. He had real love—a patient and waiting love. There is an insightful verse in Genesis which says, "Jacob served seven years for Rachel, and they seemed to him but a few days for the love he had to her."[2]

If your love is impetuous, if your love has to move fast, if you have to tie the knot right away, then something is wrong. God's love will wait for God's timing. Probably 85 percent of the counseling at our church is marital counseling. Of that 85 percent at least half are about problems that came about because the couple rushed into the marriage commitment and made a bond between them without building the proper foundation. They weren't willing to wait for God's perfect person or His perfect timing. They took things into their own hands and paid the price for years because they weren't willing to wait upon the Lord.

Rushing into marriage without the proper timing is like building a house without a proper foundation, or not putting the wiring in the right way, or not installing the plumbing according to the building code. Later when you're living in that house you may have a fire because of the faulty wiring. Or you may rupture a pipe and flood your newly laid carpeting because the plumbing wasn't installed properly. It's the same way when you rush into marriage without laying the proper foundation.

Every marriage, no matter how much a couple is in love and how committed they think they are to each other, will have difficulties, trials, and hardships. That's why I think a minimum of a year is necessary for each couple to really get to know each other before marriage. This way they are able to see each other in every conceivable situation—in stress, in difficulties, in good times as well as bad—and see how that mate weathers each situation. That's the person with whom you will spend the rest of your life, and you need to know those things up front.

If you see that a flower is almost ready to bloom and you pluck it prematurely, you may kill it before it reaches its full potential. If you take cookies out of the oven before they are completely done just because you're hungry, you're only going to have globs of dough. Taking a relationship into the bond of marriage before it's ready, you can do indescribable destruction. So we must not only wait to find out who God wants us to marry, but we must also wait to find out *His right timing*.

Moses in a Hurry

A classic example of God's timing is the story

of Moses. God had called Moses to deliver the children of Israel out of Egypt. One day he found an Egyptian beating one of the Jews. Moses looked to his left and looked to his right and then killed the Egyptian because he wanted to be the deliverer of God's people. But the problem was that he was doing it in his own strength, not God's.

The next day Moses saw two Hebrews arguing. Thinking that he was God's deliverer, he went up to them and tried to stop the argument. One of them turned and said to him, "Are you going to kill us as you did the Egyptian yesterday?" At that point Moses realized he was in trouble. The word was out. Moses knew that Pharaoh would have him arrested, and so he fled into obscurity for 40 years.

The problem with Moses wasn't that it was God's will for him to lead the children of Israel out of bondage; the problem was Moses' timing. Moses pushed ahead of God's timing and did more destruction than good. But 40 years later, when God's call came to Moses, then he found great success.

The same is true for you.

Proverbs 3:5,6 says, "Trust in the Lord with all thine heart, and lean not unto thine own understanding. In all thy ways acknowledge Him, and He shall direct thy paths." That's telling you not to connive. Don't try to figure out ways to make something work that wasn't meant to work. do you want God to direct your paths? Do you want to know who the mate is that God has picked out for you? Then trust in Him with all your heart. Don't lean on your own understanding. And acknowledge Him in all your ways.

1. Matthew 10:29-31.
2. Genesis 29:20.

3

God's Divine Design

Let's go back to the beginning of the Bible and read about the first marriage. In Genesis 2 we read that God created Adam and placed him in the Garden of Eden. But God did not create Eve at the same time He created Adam. Genesis 2:18 says, "And the Lord God said, 'It is not good that the man should be alone; I will make a helpmeet for him.' " The word "helpmeet" means simply a helper, or, as another translator defines it, "Someone coming to rescue another."

29

Before I was married, I lived in Newport Beach, and I would often walk on the beach at night. That's the worst thing you can do when you're lonely. I felt so sorry for myself. I was starting to make a major production about wanting to get married. But the Lord was trying to tell me that He was with me. I would say, "Lord, I know You're with me, but the problem is that You're invisible. I can't put my arm around You." But I learned that Jesus is truly a Friend who sticks closer than a brother. At those times when I was loneliest, God made Himself real to me in a special way. Our friendship and love were so close that it is a time I look back on with great fondness.

Jesus said, "I will never leave thee nor forsake thee."[1] You are not alone. Jesus is there by your side. He wants to comfort you. He doesn't want to take away that need for a man or a woman in your life, because that's something He created. But He wants to *temporarily sustain* it until the time is right.

A Man's Need

It is not good for man to be alone, God said. "And out of the ground the Lord God formed every beast of the field and every fowl of the air, and brought them unto Adam to see what he would call them; and whatever Adam called every living creature, that was its name. And Adam gave names to all cattle, and to the fowl of the air, and to every beast of the field; but for Adam there was not found a helpmeet for him."[2]

Adam gave names to all the animals, but that didn't fill the emptiness inside him. For God had put inside Adam, as He puts inside every man, a desire to be fulfilled by that woman created for him.

So we read, "And the Lord God caused a deep sleep to fall upon Adam, and he slept; and He took of of his ribs, and closed up the flesh instead; and the rib which the Lord God had taken from man made He a woman, and brought her unto the man. And Adam said, 'This is now bone of my bones and flesh of my flesh; she shall be called Woman, because she was taken out of Man.' Therefore shall a man leave his father and his mother, and shall cleave unto his wife, and they shall be one flesh. And they were both naked, the man and his wife, and were not ashamed."[3]

Woman is a part of man. An old Hebrew proverb says, "Woman wasn't made from man's head to be above him, or from his feet to be walked on by him, but from his rib to be close to his heart." This is where God designed the woman to be—close to the man's heart.

God took something out of man and from it made woman. From that point on, the part missing in Adam was to be filled with that woman through marriage. God ordained marriage and He blesses it.

Leaving and Cleaving

I want you to notice two words: "leave" and "cleave." The word "cleave" literally means "glue together." God wants to take two people from their separate families and glue them together. That's why this bond must be considered with the utmost prayer and not be moved into too quickly. The couples becomes one flesh. The reason that divorce is so tragic is because it takes something that is one and rips it in two. Though people talk about surviving their divorces, I have never met a divorced person who has not experienced a great deal of pain and anguish. Divorce is something you don't even want to consider.

Divorce is one of the most destructive forces in our country today. No one can understand its anguish and pain unless he has been through it. As a child of divorced parents, I know the pain and rejection, the confusion and guilt that I felt as a result of going through their divorce. When two people have become one through marriage and are then divorced, it's like taking a piece of cloth and ripping it right down the middle. Both pieces are left with threads dangling loose. How can that be done in humans without causing indescribable pain? It's not a wound that heals quickly. The scars remain for many years. Divorce is just not worth the misery and heartache it always brings.

One reason why marriages are failing so often is because people go into the marriage relationship saying, "If it doesn't work out, we can always get a divorce." That is wrong. If you are a child of God and you want God's will, you do not enter into a relationship with divorce as an option. Sometimes I think the word "divorce" should be removed from our vocabulary as Christians. It is used too freely. We should run from it.

When we think of divorce as an option, we are not making a true commitment. That is why preventive steps must be made in the beginning, when the foundation is built on Jesus Christ and the man and woman strive to obey everything the Scriptures teach on marriage. Then their chances of divorce drop drastically.

A lot of people are saying, "Why get married? Let's just live together." That's very popular these days. The 1980 census report says that the number of unmarried couples living together rose 300 percent in ten years! Those living together think, "We can do all the things that married couples do in marriage. So why get married?" The truth is that you don't even get a good idea of what marriage is about by living together, because you are not one unit. That's what the word "cleave" is all about. It is the cohesive bond of marriage. It's not sharing the toothbrush together, or having sexual relations (though that is a part of oneness), or having the same last name, or even having children. It's when God spiritually binds and grafts you together and makes you one.

God won't bless a relationship where two people are just living together outside the bond of marriage.

True Oneness

It's hard for someone who is not married to understand what true oneness is, as God declares it. It happens when a man and a woman come together not only physically and emotionally, but also spiritually. The primary essence of that oneness is a spiritual bond that God puts between them.

This is the primary area where Satan attacks a marriage. The enemy tries to sever the oneness between a couple by decreasing their desire to communicate. Any enemy knows that the best way to destroy a soldier is to break communication with his commanding officer as well as the other troops. In the same way in the spiritual war that we fight, Satan tries to break off communication with our commanding Officer, the Captain of our salvation, Jesus Christ, causing us not to listen to Him and obey His directives. Then he will try to sever the communication between a man and his wife and to isolate them from each other.

This is how it often happens: One partner will do something that makes the other angry. Yet nothing is said. What started as a minor offense builds and builds inside until a gigantic brick wall has been assembled. Finally the person explodes and makes a major production out of what could have been resolved originally through a simple discussion.

That is why couples must constantly communicate with each other. It is a vital part of oneness. Communicating is learning to talk to each other. But it is also learning to *listen*. James tells us that every person must be quick to listen, slow to speak, and slow to anger.[4] If we would spend more time listening than talking, we would get in a lot less trouble.

Knowing Your Mate

In 1 Peter 3:7 husbands are told to live with their wives according to knowledge. The word "live" in the original Greek literally means "to dwell down with and be aligned to." That is difficult for many men. They don't want to "dwell down with" their wives. They want their wives to adapt themselves to *their* lifestyle, running around with all of *their* friends, doing whatever interests *them*. But they don't want to adapt themselves to their wives' lifestyle.

Living with your wife also means to be aligned together. I don't know how I do it, but I have a knack for getting my cars out of alignment. I can drive out of a tire store after an alignment and within a few blocks run over a pothole or hit a curb, and my tires are out of alignment again. What that means is that one tire is pulling one direction while the other is pulling a different way. As a result, my tires wear out faster. What I need to do is align my tires again so that they all are going in the same direction. In the marriage relationship, to be aligned means that we are both moving in the same direction. "Can two walk together unless they be agreed?" Scripture asks.[5] Going the same direction in life is an important aspect of oneness.

We are told to live with our wives according to *knowledge*. The word "knowledge" means that we need to *know* her. Many men don't take time to get to know their wives—to know their strengths, weaknesses, hopes, aspirations, and fears. This is all a part of that oneness that can only take place when a man and a woman make a total and complete commitment to the Lord Jesus Christ and to each other.

This oneness also shows itself physically when children are born. A child bears the traits and features of both parents. Perhaps someone comes up to your child and says to the father, "He has your eyes and your wife's nose." Then when he screams and yells and throws a tantrum, you might say, "He has his mother's temper." That child is a reflection of both parents.

No Trial Runs

I believe that the real reason people live together outside of marriage is that they don't want to commit themselves. They call it a "trial run." But if you are a child of God and He shows you the person you are to marry, you don't need a trial run. He's already figured out all the details for you.

Some people say, "Marriage is just signing a piece of paper, and that's unnecessary. We'll just go stand under a tree and ask God to bless us and everything will be okay." No, it isn't okay. Again, they don't know what it means to be as one. Marriage is leaving and cleaving.

The leaving part is a public statement in which you say to anyone who attends your wedding, "I am committing myself to this man or this woman. I am planning to spend the rest of my life with this person." When you've stated it publicly, you have to stick to it. It's a promise. That's why people are reluctant to get married: They're afraid to make that commitment.

If you want to experience God's very best in your life, then concentrate on knowing God first. Let Him pick your mate for you. Be patient for His timing. When the timing is right, leave your family and cleave to your mate in marriage.

1. Hebrews 13:5.
2. Genesis 2:19,20.
3. Genesis 2:21-25.
4. James 1:19.
5. Amos 3:3.

4

The Big Date

Finally we get to the subject of dating. The Bible doesn't say anything specifically about dating. I've read a lot of Christian books that talk about it. They say things like, "What a Chistian should do on a date: First, pick her up. Open the car door for her. Wait for her to get in. Then close it. Just remember to make sure she's all the way in the car first!" I've read books that suggest going to an ice cream social and avoiding "Lovers' Lane." But that type of advice doesn't meet today's needs.

I realize that two believers are under a lot of pressure when they go out on a date. Dating is an activity peculiar to our culture. It was not part of the Jewish culture when the Bible was written. Instead, most marriages were arranged, as we saw with Isaac and Rebekah. Usually a couple was paired from the same town and tribe in which they grew up. And that tradition is still practiced in many cultures around the world today.

Under the Pressure

As a teenager, I was a horrible dater. I only dated a handful of times and I hated it every time. I always felt pressure to impress the girl I was dating. One time I took a girl to a nice restaurant. When we sat down, I couldn't think of one thing to say. After a few minutes of stumbling, I managed to come up with, "Isn't this a nice restaurant?"

"No, I think it stinks," she answered. It seemed like all I could say after that were dumb things, and then I'd think to myself, "Why did I say that?"

When two Christians date, I don't think they should have such problems. The reason is because of what you have in common. **The best way I've found to break the ice is to start your date with prayer.** That's not what most couples normally do on dates, but that's what you *should* do.

We've been talking about being the person God wants us to be. We've talked about seeking Him first. What better way to do that than by prayer? It's the best way to take care of those nervous feelings. The Apostle Paul wrote, "Be careful [or anxious] for nothing, but in everything by prayer and supplication with thanksgiving let your requests be made known unto God. And the peace of God, which passeth all understanding, shall keep your hearts and minds through Christ Jesus."[1]

Drawing Near to God

James tells us, "Draw near to God and He will draw near to you."[2] I believe I can get to know a person better by spending ten minutes in prayer with him than by spending two hours in conversation. By seeing what his attitude is when approaching the heavenly Father, I learn what his relationship with God is like.

And that should be our focus in dating. Our ultimate purpose as Christians is to draw closer to God. Therefore, in a dating relationship, the first thing you want to know about is your partner's relationship to Christ. If the other person isn't attempting to draw closer to God, then how will he help you draw closer to God? And that doesn't mean just going to church. A lot of us can put on a good show in church. But then we get in our cars and peel rubber out of the parking lot and run over people—"Sorry, brother, here's your arm back!" So when you get with a person away from spiritual surroundings, you find out what he's really like.

I suggest that a part of every date should be some form of spiritual activity. It's great to go out and have fun. Have dinner together. Or go witnessing. Or take part in a church activity. Then, if nothing else comes of your date, at least you have had some fellowship as Christians and you have helped each other grow a little closer to the Lord.

The Inequality Trap

What about dating unsaved people? I get asked this question all the time. Girls are usually the ones who ask. "No Christian guys ever asks me out," they complain. "They're all jerks anyway. But there are so many cute guys in the world. I know this one really good-looking guy and he asked me out. I'm going to witness to him. When he tries to kiss me, I'm going to stick a Bible right in his mouth."

I've heard that story many times. They *do* go out, and he does try to kiss her—and she kisses him back. The next thing you know, she's falling in love with him. And then I'm asked the question, "Greg, is it okay to marry a non-Christian?"

The Word of God says, "Be not unequally yoked together with unbelievers, for what fellowship hath righteousness with unrighteousness, and what communion hath light with darkness?"[3]

God makes it perfectly clear that a believer is not to marry an unbeliever. If that's true, then why date an unbeliever? You don't share any common spiritual ground.

Usually an unbeliever draws a believer away from the Lord. I've seen many girls fall for some guy who says, "I believe in God. I'll go to church with you."

"What about tonight?" she might ask.

"No, not tonight. Let's go to this party. On our next date we'll go to church."

The next date comes and she says, "Let's go to church."

But he says, "I'm not feeling up to it tonight. Let's just go over to my place and watch TV. We'll go some other time."

And soon she's snared in a trap because her affections are wrapped up in that man, and she's drawn away from the Lord. That's why I highly recommend that you do some spiritual activities on every date. Pray together. Study the Word together. In that way you build in each other things that will last for eternity, even if nothing else comes of your relationship.

1. Philippians 4:6,7.
2. James 4:8.
3. 2 Corinthians 6:14.

5

Qualities That Count

Women, what do you look for in a man? Guys, what do you look for in a girl? We've said that God wants to provide you with a mate. How will you recognize him or her? And how can you prepare yourself to be that perfect mate?

Today so much emphasis is placed on how a person looks. If you believe the commercials, women have to be thin, style their hair in a certain way, and wear only the right kind of designer clothes. This peer pressure of external appearances extends down into the junior high level and even into the elementary schools.

Men as well as women constantly receive this kind of influence from the world, so they start thinking, "The kind of girl I want to marry has to be five-feet-six, blond-haired, blue-eyed..." and so on.

The Right Standards

What does the Bible have to say about this? The Bible says to wives in 1 Peter 3, "Your beauty should not come from outward adornment, such as braided hair and the wearing of gold jewelry and fine clothes. Instead, it should be that of your inner self, the unfading beauty of a gentle and quiet spirit, which is of great worth in God's sight."[1]

Men, there's nothing wrong with admiring an attractive woman. But you should take the longest look at her inner spirit. Women, this should be your goal—to have a gentle and quiet spirit. This doesn't mean that you go out with a bag over your head. In fact, some girls need to be a little more concerned about their outward appearance. This is an element that we can't forget altogether. On the other hand, I know of many girls who spend two hours in front of the mirror before they ever leave their home. There's nothing wrong with wanting to look nice, but don't you think God deserves at least equal time? Do you spend as much time in prayer as you spend in front of a mirror? Ultimately, it's your *inward* beauty that will shine brighter than your makeup or your clothes. So it's important to work at least as hard on your spiritual makeup as your physical makeup.

Proverbs 31:10 says, "Who can find a virtuous woman? For her price is far above rubies." A virtuous woman is a godly woman. The rest of Proverbs 31 goes on to tell us all the things this woman does and concludes with this line: "Favor is deceitful and beauty is vain, but a woman who fears the Lord shall be praised."[2] When you radiate Jesus Christ, guys will be drawn to you like a magnet.

Religious Fanatic?

In fact, that's how I became a Christian. One day in high school I noticed a girl on campus. She was attractive, though not a beauty queen. Yet there was something about her that made me think, "I've got to know her." I watched her every day, and when I finally saw her talking to Mark, one of my friends, I went over real casually and said, "Hi, Mark, how are you doing?" As we talked, I looked down at her notebook and saw one of those black books with gold pages. I was disappointed. "Oh, no, she's a religious fanatic!'' I thought. ''What a waste!''

Then I realized that I really didn't know anything about so-called religious fanatics, or ''Jesus freaks,'' as we often called them. All I knew was that I didn't want to be one. One afternoon a few days later I found this girl sitting among a big circle of people. I walked over and saw that it was a Christian meeting, so I sat down to find out what it was all about. After some singing, a man started sharing the gospel, and as I listened to him I no longer was thinking about the girl. That afternoon, when he gave an invitation, I came to know Jesus Christ.

Do you see how important this is? This girl never spoke a word to me, but it was her inward beauty, caused by the Lord, that drew me to her. When you radiate the love of Jesus Christ, guys see it. That's why they ask you to go out with them. It's because you're different. You're attractive *inwardly*.

Looking for a Man

On the other side, what should girls look for in a man? It's basically the same thing. You are looking for a man who exudes spiritual character. To understand what that means, let's look at Ephesians 5:25: "Husbands, love your wives, even as Christ also loved the church and gave Himself for it.'' This means that men should be like Jesus

Christ. He is their example. This is far more important than what a man looks like, or the kind of job he has, or the model of car he drives.

Women, ask yourself this question about any man you date: "Is he a spiritual leader?" Does he take the lead in spiritual matters, like prayng with you? Is he someone you can respect because he's growing in the Lord? Is he the kind of man who doesn't just say "praise the Lord" in the pew, but says it out on the streets, too? Does he serve the Lord not only in church but also in day-to-day living? Is he a man who lives an uncompromising life for Jesus Christ?

I think it is so very important that we be looking for these qualities in the men and women we're around. Let's help each other develop the inner qualities that will really count for a lifetime, long after physical beauty has faded, and on into eternity.

1. 1 Peter 3:3,4 (NIV).
2. Proverbs 31:30.

6

The Subject of Love

The word "love" is used so freely that it is difficult to know what it really means. We use it to say "I love my wife" and "I love my dog" and "I love tacos." Obviously a man doesn't love his wife the same way he loves tacos—at least I hope not. The word "love" has a number of different meanings.

If we took a poll of 200 people off the street, asking them to define "love," we would probably get 200 different definitions. I looked up "love" in a dictionary, and it said, "A profoundly tender, passionate affection. A feeling of warm personal attatchment." It went on to say, "Sexual desire or its gratification."

What Kind of Love?

An expression we hear often is "falling in love." Most of us have experienced this at least once. When you fall in love with someone, you find yourself constantly thinking about that person. You want to know his feelings about everything. Sometimes it affects your appetite— some people eat more, some less!

Sometimes what we call love is simply infatuation. This kind of "love" is where you meet someone and you worship the ground on which he or she walks. You don't look at him realistically. Sometimes we call this "puppy love." (The problem with puppy love is that it often leads to a dog's life!)

Most of us look forward to falling in love because it really is a great thing. And it's something that God has designed within us. It's not something evil or wicked. Kept in the proper balance, it's something truly beautiful.

In order to talk about love, we need to define it. If you think you're in love right now, you need to understand what's going on inside yourself. I want you to know what real love is.

In the Greek language, in which the New Testament was originally written, there are four basic words for love. One is *eros*, which is love on the physical plane. Another is *phileo*, which is love on the emotional plane. The third is *storgae*, which is a variation of *phileo* referring to the love within a family. Then there is the highest form of love available, the word *agape*. It is a love that comes from God and motivates a person to give rather than to get. When you read the word "love" in the New Testament, it usually is a translation of the word *agape*.

We will talk more about *agape* love later. Right now I want to address physical love or the Greek word *eros*. That's probably a word you've heard before, and it probably conjures up all sorts of dark thoughts. Generally we see this word portrayed on those seedy little bookstores that plug pornographic publications. You might say, "I don't want anything to do with that kind of love." But *eros* is not completely bad.

Good and Bad Sex

In fact, there is definitely a place for *eros* or physical love. Often Christians are afraid to deal with the subject of sex. But God addresses it clearly in His Word, so I don't think we need to run away from it. Sex is something that God created. It's beautiful when experienced in the way God intended for it to be enjoyed.

If I were to go out in my garden, pick up a handful of rich, dark soil, and rub it into a brand-new white carpet, the owner of that carpet would not be very pleased. That beautiful soil looked great out in the garden because it belonged there, but when I put that soil on the carpet, it suddenly was out of place. It became dirt because it was no longer where it belonged.

Sex within the realm of marriage is blessed. Hebrews 13:4 says, "Marriage is honorable in all, and the bed undefiled." God made sex and He knows how to bless it. It's difficult for us to understand that God can bless a sexual relationship, but it is true. If I were having difficulty with my car, I wouldn't go down to the supermarket boxboy and ask him to take a look under the hood. I'd go to a certified auto shop. In the same way, if you're having difficulty in a sexual relationship, you should go to the One who created it—God.

Sex outside the marital relationship is called many things, such as "making love" and "having an affair." It's dressed up with pretty words and made to sound glamorous. But God does not bless it. The thing that was once beautiful within its place suddenly becomes a destructive force that wipes you out spiritually. In some ways sex is like fire. Used properly, it can warm you and be a source of comfort. But taken outside its proper place, it can become a ravaging inferno that destroys everything in its path. The Scripture says, "Can a man take fire in his bosom, and his clothes not be burned?" (Proverbs 6:27).

God blesses the sexual relationship within the marital bond. One way He blesses it is that there is absolutely no guilt attached to it. In marriage there are not questions like "Is this right?" or "Is this acceptable?" Many people say they don't feel guilt as a result of having sexual relations outside marriage. But they really aren't telling the truth. Deep down in their hearts they are aware that they are breaking the commandments of God. But when two people are married, there is a freedom and openness with each other and the assurance that God is pleased with their relationship.

The Sex Pressure

Today young people are facing tremendous pressure to have sexual experiences. Movies constantly push the idea of sex among consenting adults. Songs on the radio tell how great sex is. Magazines show models in provocative clothing and poses. Then in school your friends give you a hard time if you haven't had a sexual experience by a certain age. It's hard for you if you are a Christian because you know what God wants you to do, yet you're under a lot of pressure to do what everyone else says is acceptable.

A 15-year-old girl was quoted in an article about teenage sex by *Newsweek* magazine as saying, "I wasn't able to handle the pressure. I was part of a group of people in junior high school that was into partying, hanging out and drinking. I started to have sex with my boyfriend and it was a real downer. It was totally against what I was, but it was important to be part of a group. Everybody was having sex."[1]

I would venture to say that most people, like this young girl, when they have their first sexual experience find out that it's not as great as they thought it would be. A recent report stated that 43 percent of all boys and 31 percent of all girls in the United States lose their virginity by the age of 16. Yet despite the steady rise in teenage sexuality, *most adolescents don't enjoy sex.* Girls often feel guilt, sadness, shame, or regret, and are more likely to evidence conflicting or negative feelings about themselves as a result. The fact is that sex is one of the most overrated things on earth. But people won't admit it. They go back to their friends and say it was just great, even when it wasn't great. They say it to impress each other.

The article in *Newsweek* goes on to say that "50 percent of the nation's 10.3 million young women age 15 to 19 have had premarital sex. The percentage has nearly doubled since Zelnik and Kanter began their surveys in 1971.''[2] The article also states, "Statistics in a 1977 study show that 600,000 unwed teenagers were giving birth each year, with the sharpest increase among those under 14. Venereal disease is rampant among adolescents, accounting for 25 percent of the 1 million reported gonorrhea cases every year.''[3]

Paying the Penalty

That's one of the problems with violating God's laws—there is a penalty to pay. The Bible says that sin is pleasurable for a season,[4] and that "there is a way which seemeth right unto a man, but the end therof are the ways of death.''[5]

Recently my wife, Cathe, planted some new flowers. The next morning we discovered that they had been consumed by a small army of hungry snails. So Cathe got some snail repellent and sprinkled this bright, reddish powder in a circle around some newer flowers she had planted. I've never thought of snails as exceptionally intelligent creatures, but I never thought they would be stupid enough to go out of their way to consume this poisonous powder. But sure enough, the next morning there were about 50 of them lying dead next to those flowers!

I wondered what must have gone through their little snail brains prior to their demise. Perhaps one snail cautiously oozed up to the bright powder and looked it over for a moment while the others waited about 20 inches back. Then he bent down and took a small bite and was absolutely enraptured with the most incredible, pleasurable taste he had ever known. He called back to the others, "Comrade snails, this is the most delicious, the most—" Suddenly that snail dropped over dead. Now you would think that at this point the other snails would learn from the one snail's mistake. But no, they couldn't line up quick enough for a taste of this delicious powder. They each enjoyed a brief moment of ecstasy, then died.

Death of the Innocent

That's how it is with sex outside marriage. Girls are the primary victims in this area. A guy might say, "If you really love me, if you really care, show me by making love with me." The girl wants someone to be tender and affectionate toward her. She believes the only way this guy will care for her is to give in to his desire. So the guy takes away that precious thing from her—her virginity. And often she finds that she gets nothing in return.

Nothing, that is, except perhaps an unwanted pregnancy. And then she has a decision to make: "Should I go ahead and be pregnant and let all my friends see that?" she thinks. "I can't do that. It's too embarrasing and humiliating." So what is the alternative? Abortion. Kill the baby. Since 1973, 12 million innocent babies have been systematically destroyed by legal abortion.[6]

That's how dangerous sex outside marriage can be. One little feeling of lust and physical attraction can result in the murder of an unborn child who doesn't have any ability to choose. Sin always has a snowball effect, and many people, even Christians, who experiment in this area of sex and then get married thinking they will have no problems are in for a big surprise. I've counseled with enough couples to see that, even years after they were married, they still have difficulties because they disobeyed God in this area.

That's why you must nip it in the bud. If you aren't married and you're involved in sexual relations with a guy or a girl, draw the line right now. Don't go any further. If you haven't had sex, don't start until you're married.

1. "The Games Teen-Agers Play," *Newsweek*, Sept. 1, 1981, p. 48.
2. Ibid.
3. Ibid.
4. Hebrews 11:25.
5. Proverbs 14:12

6. God forbid that you should get into such a dilemma. But if you do, don't even consider abortion. Rather, plan on keeping the child and raising him or her yourself, or place the baby for adoption. There are countless beautiful Christian couples who would be thrilled to adopt the child.

7

The Bible and Sex

The Bible has numerous examples of people who experimented with "sexual freedom" only to regret it afterward. Solomon was a man who had 700 wives and 300 concubines. This means that he had 1000 women at his disposal any time he wanted them. At the end of his life, after he had pursued all the pleasure any man could ever want, he wrote this conclusion: "I said in my heart, I will prove thee with mirth; therefore enjoy pleasure.... And whatever my eyes desired I kept not from them; I withheld not my heart from any joy.... Then I looked on all the works that my hands had wrought, and on the labor that I had labored to do; and, behold all was vanity and vexation of spirit, and there was no profit under the sun."[1]

David's Second Look

Solomon's father, King David, was another man who paid a severe penalty for his disobedience in the area of sexual restraint. It all started one day when David should have been out with his army fighting a battle. Late in the afternoon he went up to his roof and from there saw a beautiful woman taking a bath. This is a classic case of temptation. I think it's possible that David knew that Bathsheba bathed openly at this time of day. And I think that perhaps Bathsheba also knew about David's walks on his housetop and made sure she was in the right place at the right time.

Girls seem to know how to get guys to look at them. There are certain things they can wear (or not wear!) to quickly get attention. Christian girls need to be very careful in this area.

On David's part, there was little he could do about that first look. All of us see things we don't necessarily want or plan to see. The problem isn't with the *first* look but the *second*. That's usually when trouble starts. I read about a man who was driving down a street when he saw a girl walking totally naked down the sidewalk. He couldn't take his eyes off her, and he ran off the road and was killed. That man couldn't avoid the first look. But he could have avoided the second.

So David couldn't avoid the first look—there was Bathsheba. What he should have done was to say, "Oh God, help me," and to hightail it out of there as quick as his two legs could carry him. But instead he looked a second time. Then he lusted within his mind and his heart. Then he arranged for Bathsheba to be brought to him, and as a result of their sexual relations she became pregnant. Now he was really in a bind. But, rather than confess to the Lord, "I have sinned; forgive me," David tried to cover up his sin. But the more he tried to hide it, the worse it got. Eventually he ended up having an innocent man—Bathsheba's own husband—murdered.

Paying and Paying

Now look at the consequences of David's lust. David confessed his sin before God but still paid a heavy price. God said, "Behold, I will raise up evil against thee out of thine own house, and I will take thy wives before thine eyes and give them to thy neighbor, and he shall lie with thy wives in the sight of this sun. For thou didst it secretly, but I will do this thing before all Israel and before the sun.''[2]

From that point on David had nothing but trouble. First, the child of Bathsheba died seven days after he was born. Later one of David's sons committed incest with one of his daughters. Then his favorite son, Absalom, led a rebellion against him. Then Absalom took ten of David's concubines. Finally Absalom was killed. David's life was never the same after his sin.

All of this happened to David *after* God forgave him. God will forgive you if you sin in this area, but you must realize that you will still pay some serious consequences. It doesn't just stop when you say, "God, I'm sorry." You may have an unwanted child as a result of your mistake. You will damage your witness to your friends in the place where you work or go to school. In some way or another it will have ongoing repercussions.

The Apostle Paul writes in his letter to the Galatians, "Be not deceived; God is not mocked [outwitted or evaded]: for whatsoever a man soweth, that shall he also reap. For he that soweth in his flesh shall of the flesh reap corruption [or rottenness]; but he that soweth to the Spirit shall reap life everlasting."[3] We must realize that every sin has its consequence, even as every sowing has its reaping. If a farmer planted weeds, he wouldn't reap corn but weeds.

The Creeping Virus

Today 20 million Americans are reaping a bitter result of sexual looseness in the form of a venereal disease called herpes. Herpes is a viral infection that is transmitted during sex, and no cure has been found for it. The word "herpes" comes from a Greek word meaning "to creep."

That's just what this virus does. It crawls along internal nerve pathways until it reaches the outer skin layer and erupts into painful blisters. One person described it this way: "It's like someone putting a soldering iron to your skin." Another person said, "The pain was excruciating. I thought I'd die. I couldn't lie down, sit, or even walk."

This infection not only causes great pain physically, emotionally, and psychologically, but it destroys marriages as well. In a monogamous relationship, the unsuspecting person who picks up herpes from a partner is hit with a double whammy—evidence of betrayal plus a lifelong disease as a memento of the event. Herpes can even be life-threatening. The evidence of cervical cancer is four times higher among women with herpes.

I was asked by the religious editor of a major metropolitan newspaper if I thought herpes was a judgment of God on the disobedient people of the earth, like a plague in the days of Moses. I told him I thought it was more of a reaping what had been sowed. It's not that God specifically sent herpes to punish disobedient people, but rather that man brought herpes upon himself by breaking God's laws.

This disease is just another reason why we need to pay attention to God's design for our human bodies. The only way God will bless a couple sexually is when they have committed themselves to each other in the bond of marriage.

Samson's Weakness

Samson is another man in the Old Testament who had problems with sexual sin. It literally cost him his life. Samson is best-known for his long hair and great strength. His strength was in his commitment to God, which in his case was symbolized by his hair having never been cut.

But Samson had a weakness for women. One of the women he fell for was a Philistine named Delilah. Samson had had nothing but problems with Philistine women, but rather than put a distance between himself and the temptation, he toyed with it.

Delilah would come to Samson and say, "If you really love me, tell me the secret of your strength." What's interesting about this story is that every time Samson gave her an answer, it came a little closer to the truth. First he told her that if she bound him with seven new ropes, he would lose all his strength. So she did that and then called out, "The Philistines are upon you." Samson easily broke those ropes and got free, but you would think that at this point he would realize the trap.

Delilah came to him again begging for the secret of his strength. This time he replied that if she wove his hair and nailed it to the ground, he would lose all his strength. Sure enough, when he went to sleep, she wove his hair and nailed it to the ground, then called the Philistines. Samson jumped up, ripped the beam out of the ground, and escaped.

Certainly at this point you would think that Samson would understand what was happening. Couldn't he see what was going on? Yes, he could. Yet here is the trickery of sin: It deceives you. A person on the outside can say, "You fool, what are you doing? Don't you see you can ruin your marriage and destroy your wife and children by this act of adultery?" But that person is deceived by sin. He thinks he is in control of the situation when he really isn't.

Finally Delilah said, "Samson, everyone's laughing at me." For days she bugged him until he finally told her the truth: "Shave my head and I'll lose my strength." This time when she said,

"The Philistines are upon you," Samson didn't get away. They grabbed him, gouged out his eyes, and forced him to grind meal as a slave. And of course he ultimately died a premature death as a result of sin.

Listen to the Warning

Perhaps you're caught right now in a relationship that is not of God. You're in a sexual relationship outside marriage. God is saying to you, "Get out of it right now!" If you don't obey Him after reading this, and keep on doing it, then it's your own fault. Don't say to God, "You didn't warn me!" He's warning you right now!

As we live in these lasts days waiting for the Lord to return, the areas of sexual temptation are going to get worse. If your life isn't right with Jesus Christ, it's going to be tough.

Jesus said, "As the days of Noah were, so shall also the coming of the Son of man be."[4] One of the primary sins in the time of Noah was sexual perversion. As I look back over history, I cannot find a time that is more perverted than right now.

If you think that when you get married your temptations in the area of sex will go away, you're mistaken. Sometimes when you marry, sexual temptation gets worse. You can never be 100 percent free from sexual temptation. So that's why

we must next discuss how to deal with that
temptation.

1. Ecclesiastes 2:1,10,11.
2. 2 Samuel 12:11,12.
3. Galatians 6:7,8.
4. Matthew 24:37.

8

Dealing With Temptation

⤜❧❦❧⤛

What can you do to protect yourself in the area of sexual temptation? Let's say you have a girlfriend and you find her very attractive. In fact you very much want to be close to her, to hold her, to kiss her. So you might ask what many young people have asked me: "How far can we go as Christians?" The very fact that someone asks me that question shows me that he is on dangerous ground. I have seen some churches where they literally have rules that say a man cannot touch a woman and they have to remain so many inches apart from each other. On the other hand, I've met Christians who have what they call "liberty," and they feel they can do just about anything they want to. In the Scriptures we find a balance between these two extremes.

Freedom's Guidelines

The Apostle Paul lays out some "principles for affection" in Colossians. He doesn't give us "ten commandments for affection." Rather, he gives us something better. He gives us freedom—freedom to serve God. Paul wrote in 1 Corinthians that "all things are lawful unto me, but all things are not expedient; all things are lawful, but I will not be brought under the power of any."[1]

One question to ask yourself if you are getting involved physically is, "Do you have the ability to turn off your passion at the drop of a hat?" If you're honest, the answer is no. You are under its power. It's a little like a fuse on a bomb: Once you light it, it's hard to stop.

So on the one hand, we've been given liberty. However, Paul cautions us not to use freedom "for an occasion to the flesh."[2] So what is our freedom for? What are we to do with our affections? The answer is in Colossians 3: "If ye then be risen with Christ, seek those things which are above, where Christ sitteth on the right hand of God. Set your affection on things above, not on things on the earth.''[3]

The first thing he says is that if you are risen with Christ—meaning you are a Christian—then set your affection on things above and not on things below. To set your affection means to ''set your mind'' or ''to think constantly.'' Paul says we shouldn't be asking questions like ''How far can we go?'' but rather ''What can I do to bring honor to Jesus Christ?'' and ''How can I show my love for Him?''

If you are living on the borderline, trying to see how much you can get away with and still be a Christian, you're on thin ice. Sooner or later that ice is going to break. But if you are walking in the power of the Spirit and thinking constantly about the way God wants you to live, then you will ''not fulfill the lust of the flesh.''[4]

Death to Sin

The reason Paul tells us to be thinking about the things of God rather than the things of earth is because we are dead to the old life we lived in the flesh, and our lives are ''hidden with Christ in God.''[5] Therefore Paul commands us in Colossians 3:5, ''Mortify...your members which are upon the earth.'' The word ''mortify'' means "put to death or deprive of power." It means to deprive your physical desire of its power. God doesn't want to eliminate your desires altogether. But He wants them to be bridled for the time being. One day He will allow you to have a fulfillment in that physical area. Right now He wants you to focus on Him and let Him sustain you.

If you are walking close to Jesus Christ, spending time with Him in prayer and in His Word, then you are going to grow spiritually strong. If you are spending time toying and playing with temptation, then you are going to grow strong in your old nature, and your spiritual life will become weak. The two cannot coexist. It's a constant battle. Either you're growing strong in the spirit or you're growing strong in the flesh. Either you're growing closer to the Lord or you're falling away from the Lord. It's one or the other.

There is never a time when we can "take a vacation" from spiritual growth without disastrous results. Spiritual growth is an ongoing lifestyle. Only through being changed more day by day into the image of Jesus do we find freedom from sin.

I was talking to an employee of Disneyland who told me that the famous amusement park is involved in a constant beautification process. Most visitors to Disneyland take the park's clean, new look for granted. They don't realize that there is a full-time crew of painters who start at one end of the park and repaint all buildings, street lamps, signs—everything—and when they're done, they start all over again. That's how we should approach our lives—always setting our minds and affections on God and allowing Him to change us into His image.

Hit List of Evil

Paul then lists the things we should mortify or deprive of power. First is fornication. The word means "illicit sexual relations." It comes from the Greek word *pornia*. As you can see, we get the English word "pornography" from it. I've had some people tell me they think fornication means "sex without love," and because they "love" each other, their sex is acceptable to God. This is simply not true. The word includes in its scope any sex outside marriage. It even includes homosexual relationships.

Sexual vice will be judged. Galatians 5:19,21 says that those who practice "the works of the flesh [and it names fornication in the list]...shall not inherit the kingdom of God." I can't emphasize strongly enough that illicit sex will destroy your relationship with God.

Next in Colossians, Paul mentions the word "uncleanness," which means basic sexual impurities. Then he mentions "inordinate affection," which means "out-of-control passion."

There's another word the Bible uses for this—
"lasciviousness." Lasciviousness and inordinate
affection mean that you allow your passions to
grow and get out of control.

Usually temptation begins in your mind or
imagination. First you think about it. Temptations
often come at the worst times. You can be in
prayer and suddenly you're having a sexually impure thought and you're ashamed. Then you feel
guilty because Satan says, "Look at that thought,
you pervert!" But that thought is not sin. This
is where you must make a decision. Will you continue to entertain the thought, or will you draw
the line and say, "This thought is not of God,"
and reject it?

Suppose someone peddling porno magazines
came to your door and knocked. You ask, "Who
is it?" and he answers, "It's your friendly
neighborhood porno dealer." You would say
(hopefully), "Go away! I'm not even remotely in-
terested!" He might respond, "Look, there's no
obligation to buy. Just take a look through the
peephole in your door. I'll hold up one of the
magazines so you can see."

It's Your Choice

Now you have a choice. You can't make him
go away, but you can ignore him. Those who look
through the peephole are like people who, when

tempted with an impure thought, take hold of it and let it become their desire. Those who refuse to look through the peephole and ignore this temptation are the ones who have learned the secret of James 4:7: "Resist the devil, and he will flee from you."

You can be watching TV and something suggestive happens to give you a thought. You can be listening to a song on the radio and something not just suggestive but an outright blatant thought of impurity is placed in your mind. The question is, "Are you going to allow your mind to go into fantasy?" If you do, you will find yourself entering into the realm of thinking impure thoughts. This is lasciviousness, and it develops into inordinate affection, which means allowing your passions to grow out of control.

Jesus said, "Whosoever looketh on a woman to lust after her hath committed adultery with her already in his heart."[6] The world was shocked when former President Jimmy Carter said he had looked on women and lusted after them. He was just being honest. What you must do with these thoughts is to guard your minds against them. It tells us in 2 Corinthians 10:5 that men are to "cast down imaginations and every high thing that exalteth itself against the knowledge of God, and bring into captivity every thought to the obedience of Christ." So guard your mind! Guard your thoughts! Don't read things that will stimulate impure thoughts. Don't watch movies or television shows that incite impure thoughts and encourage you to lust. Back off from a relationship where you start finding those passions taking over. Put distance between yourself and these areas of weakness, lest you become a victim.

Handling Temptations

In this area of temptation there's a very important Scripture that I think every Christian should memorize. First Corinthians 10:13 says: "There hath no temptation taken you but such as is common to man; but God is faithful, who will not permit you to be tempted above that ye are able, but will with the temptation also make a way to escape, that ye may be able to bear it."

No doubt there are some temptations that are heavy duty. But I think some Christians tempt themselves by intentionally putting themselves in bad situations. James writes, "Every man is tempted when he is drawn away of his own lust and enticed."[7] A guy says to his date, "I'm going to take you home now." But along the way he comes to a dark street. "Oh, look, the street light is out!" (He doesn't mention that he put it out with a BB gun two hours before.) "Let's park here." Then nature starts taking its course and those passionate feelings start rising. Later he asks, "Oh, God, why did you let me get tempted like this?" But God answers, "Why did you drive there in the first place?" Don't blame it on God. You put yourself in that situation.

If you're on a diet, don't suggest hanging out in the local bakery. If you're a recovering alcoholic, don't hang out at bars, because you're only setting yourself up for a fall.

Sometimes a temptation is so overwhelming that there is literally only one way out—to run. If that is what it takes, then do it. In the Old Testament is the story of Joseph. The wife of his master tried to seduce him several times. One day she grabbed hold of his robe and said, "Lie with me!" Now that's temptation. Joseph was vulnerable like any other man, so he did the only thing possible: He ran. If you find youself in a situation you can't handle, then get out of there. Run.

In summary, there is no way we can avoid sexual temptation. We face it almost every day. But the Word gives us plenty of ammunition to fight it. The best answer to any temptation is in Colossians—"Keep seeking the things above." That's the key to victory.

1. 1 Corinthians 6:12.
2. Galatians 5:13.

3. Colossians 3:1,2.
4. Galatians 5:16.
5. Colossians 3:3.
6. Matthew 5:28.
7. James 1:14.

9

God's Perfect Love

We've spent a lot of time talking about one of the Greek words for love—*eros,* which is love in the physical realm. The Bible uses two of the three other Greek words for love—*phileo,* which is love in the emotional realm, and *agape,* which is love in the spiritual realm.

I believe that all three of these loves—physical, emotional, and spiritual—are important in a marriage relationship. It's important that you are physically attracted to your mate. I once talked to a young girl who was about to marry a guy, and she said, "I'm not physically attracted to him at all. In fact, I find him repulsive." I told her that I felt it was important to have a physical attraction to him as well as emotional and spiritual attraction. True oneness in marriage involves all three areas. Physical love does play an important role in the marriage relationship, though not as important as many people make it out to be.

Three Loves

Let me contrast all three loves to give you an idea of the differences. *Eros* love *takes,* wanting to give *nothing in return. Eros* is primarily a selfish love, a love that wants to get but seldom wants to give. *Phileo,* or love on the emotional plane, *takes* but also *desires to give. Phileo* desires not only to receive, but also to give back. In contrast to both *phileo* and *eros, agape* love *gives, wanting nothing in return.*

Phileo is love which comes as a result of the pleasure or delight one draws from the object of love. In contrast, *agape* springs from a sense of the preciousness of the object loved. *Agape* is primarily determined by the character of the one who loves, not the lovableness of the object. In fact, we are told to *agape* our enemies.

The most important thing to realize about *agape* love is that it is not a feeling or an emotion. We base far too much of what we call love today on our emotions. I hear people say, "We're not longer in love," or, "We fell out of love." What really happened is that they fell out of *eros,* and, to a certain degree, out of *phileo.* But the question is, "Did they ever have God's *agape* love in the first place?"

God's love is not contingent on whether your mate is pleasing you. *Agape* love continues regardless of what the other person does. That is why God says to "grow in love" rather than to "fall in love." To fall *in* love implies that you can also fall *out of* love. If you are going to have a lasting relationship, you have to build it on the foundation of God's *agape* love.

A literal definition of the word *agape* is "the absorption of every part of your being into one passion." You get the idea that *agape* is not a love that shows itself only when it is convenient, but a love that is strong regardless of circumstances.

The King James Version translates *agape* with the word "charity." Charity is a love that shows itself in good deeds. That is also a valid definition of *agape,* for it is a love that doesn't just "talk love" but also demonstrates it.

Defining Real Love

The clearest definition of God's love is found in 1 Corinthians 13. Here we are told some qualities of *agape* love, such as *agape* suffers long. This simply means that it is patient. In marriage, it means that you allow your mate to change in God's timing. Many times girls enter into a relationship thinking, "If I marry this guy, *I'm* going to *change him.*" That never works. You should be willing to accept that person as he is without the condition that he change first. Besides, as we've said before, you should concentrate on yourself, for marriage is not so much finding the right person as it is *being* the right person.

Patience in love also means that it is willing to wait, like Jacob for Rachel. Cathe and I waited almost three years until we got married. In fact, we broke up a couple of times. (I figure it's better to break up during your courtship than after you get married!) We got all the breaking up out of our systems before we said our vows.

Once after we had broken up, I participated in a tour across the country with a Christian singing group. I had determined I never wanted to be with Cathe again. But while I was on this trip, the Lord spoke to my heart and showed me that she was the one I was supposed to marry. We didn't find this out until later, but on the same day, almost at the same hour, the Lord spoke to her and showed her the same thing.

So when I came back from my trip, I immediately wanted to speak to her and tell her the good news. When I got hold of her, I blurted out that God had told me I was supposed to marry her. That scared her a bit. Although the Lord was speaking to her as well, she wasn't quite ready, and I caused her to further back away. This frustrated me, so I decided to "help God" a little bit.

One evening I really wanted to talk to her so I went to church to see her. But she was with some friends and I couldn't get alone with her. So I decided to wait at her house, and when she came home after church, then we could talk. I went over to her house and waited. It was evening and she hadn't returned yet. I started feeling kind of foolish standing out on the street corner, and I was afraid her parents would look out the window and see me. So I decided to hide in the bushes. (After all, Romeo did that, didn't he?)

Finally, after waiting about 2½ hours, her car pulled in the driveway. Excitedly I jumped out of the bushes and said, "Hi, Cathe, I've been waiting for you!" She was so scared that she ran into the house and slammed the door, and I didn't see her again that evening. After that I started bombarding her with letters and little cards and laying the romance on thick. But that didn't work either. I had to learn that love is patient, and that it waits for God's perfect timing.

We are also told in 1 Corinthians 13 that love is kind. If you are in love with a person, you should not only tell him, but you should show it with tenderness and gifts. Don't ever underestimate the effectiveness of a bouquet of flowers, or some candy, or a thoughtful little gift to the girl that you love. You may think it's corny and that people don't do it anymore. But those little token gestures do a lot to demonstrate love.

It's also good to tell someone that you love him or her. Many times we think to ourselves, "I really love that person," but we don't ever tell her. Proverbs 31 speaks of a woman whose "children rise up and call her blessed; her husband also, and he praiseth her."[1] So it is good to verbally communicate our love to the ones we care about.

We're also told that God's love does not envy; it is content with what God has given. It is easy in a relationship to become jealous. For example, if you see your girl talking to another guy, you may start having thoughts that he's moving in on you, and you're immediately filled with rage. We must be careful of envy and jealousy. Jealousy was the cause of the first murder on earth. Cain envied Abel's relationship with God.

But not envying also means that you're not intimidated by your mate's success. If a guy excels, you expect his girlfriend to be glad. But what if the girl excels? What if she gets a raise or a promotion and she starts making more money than he does? Men often find it difficult to rejoice with women on this matter. But God's love does not envy. In fact, it rejoices at the other person's success.

We are also told that God's love doesn't vaunt itself. This means that a person doesn't make a big deal of what he's doing. When you have to tell the person you love how sacrificial you are toward him and how much you give him and how wonderful you are toward him, then you are vaunting yourself. God's love doesn't do that.

We are also told that God's love is not puffed up. Literally, it is not inflated with pride. Love is not on a power trip. Many men are frustrated when their girlfriends or wives don't look to them as leaders. So they scream, yell, throw temper tantrums, and tell the women over and over, "I am the leader! I am the authority!" True authority, based on God's love, comes from humility. The classic example of that is Jesus Christ Himself. He had great authority, yet the way He achieved that authority was by humbling Himself and becoming a servant. We should do no less.

We are also told that God's love does not seek its own. This means that it is self-forgetful. It finds joy in advancing other people, not always looking out for itself, but rather for others.

Paul also mentions in 1 Corinthians that God's

love is not provoked. It is not touchy, fretful, nor resentful. It thinks no evil, meaning that it doesn't keep track of the evil done but rather of the good deeds that are done. If you have an argument and you bring up something that your husband or wife did wrong four years ago, that is provoking. So often we forget the good things and remember only the negative things. God's love only remembers the good things.

We are also told that God's love rejoices not in iniquity, but bears all things. It bears hardship, persecution, and difficulty. And it believes all things; its faith is not shattered by circumstances. It believes the best of every person. It hopes all things, and when it is disappointed, it continues to hope. It never gives up. It endures all things. God's love cannot be conquered.

Getting True Love

Now try a little test on yourself. Every place in 1 Corinthians 13 where the word "love" appears, insert your own name and see how far you get. That will help you understand the design God has for you and His *agape* love.

So you ask, "How do I get this love?" The Bible tells us, "The love of God is shed abroad in our hearts by the Holy Spirit who is given to us."[2] Jesus said, "I am the vine, ye are the branches. He that abideth in me and I in him, the same bringeth forth much fruit."³ The fruit Jesus is speaking of is the fruit of the Spirit, which according to Galatians 5:22,23 is *agape* love, described by joy, peace, longsuffering, gentleness, goodness, faith, meekness, and self-control.

The way you get God's love is by abiding in Christ. Then He sheds it abroad in your heart by His Holy Spirit. What does it mean to abide in Christ? To abide means to sink your roots deep into Jesus. Suppose you put a plant into the ground, but you don't like the way it looks in your yard, so you rip it up again and plant it somewhere else. That plant would be in such shock that it would probably never take root. It means maintaining unbroken fellowship with Him. Then the love of God will flow out of our lives.

You may think, "Does this love have any limits?" Jesus told us in John 13:34 to *agape* one another even "as I have loved you." Now ask yourself this question: "Does God's love have limits?" Does God say that if you do something wrong He will stop loving you? Not at all! God's love is consistent; it continues no matter what you do. The truth of the matter is that this kind of love melts hearts. The Scriptures tell us in 1 John 4:19, "We love Him because He first loved us." God's love can melt the greatest resistance if you will only maintain it.

One other thing I should point out is that this

agape love can grow cold. In Matthew 24 Jesus said, "Because iniquity shall abound, the love of many shall grow cold."[4] The way to keep this love fresh is by practicing it daily as we abide in Christ. It's an ongoing process. But it is ultimately most rewarding because we know that by using God's love we cannot fail in any relationship.

1. Proverbs 31:28.
2. Romans 5:5.
3. John 15:5.
4. Matthew 24:12.

10

Laying a Foundation

It is important to understand that marriage in and of itself is not something wonderful or something horrible: Marriage is neutral. It is the *participants* who make a marriage good or bad. Marriage is like a mirror: You get as much out of it as you put in. If you don't like the way you look in the morning, you can't blame the mirror. You have to do something about it yourself. What it really comes down to is commitment. Marriage can be the closest thing to heaven on earth, if we do it God's way. Or it can be the closest thing to hell on earth. The choice is ours.

Marriage is under attack as never before; modern marriage has reached the point where a happily married couple seems to be an oddity. More than 20 million U.S. couples live in desperate unhappiness. But it doesn't have to be that way. Marriage can be something strong and wonderful if we do it God's way. The reason marriages fail is because we do not obey God's standards.

Foundations for Marriage

Right now as a single person, if you are involved in a relationship with a guy or a girl, you are laying a foundation. If the Lord so leads, perhaps marriage will come out of this relationship. But whether it does or not, don't think that your days of courtship are insignificant. You are establishing habit patterns right now that will carry through into marriage. You are establishing certain ways of communicating that will continue for years to come. So *now* is the time to lay a spiritual foundation. *Now* is the time to establish good habits with your mate, such as praying together, studying the Bible together, participating in fellowship with other Christians at church, and even witnessing together.

As you lay these foundations and build upon them in years to come, your relationship will stand strong. Every marriage will have its storms. Every marriage will have its difficulties. But Jesus gave us this promise: "Whosoever heareth these sayings of mine and doeth them, I will liken him to a wise man who built his house upon a rock. The rain descended, and the floods came, and the winds blew and beat upon that house, and it fell not, for it was founded upon a rock. Everyone that heareth these sayings of mine and doeth them not shall be likened unto a foolish man who built his house upon the sand. The rain descended, and the floods came, and the winds blew and beat upon that house, and it fell; and great was the fall of it."[1]

The Best Bride and Groom

There's a beautiful analogy in Scripture in which we as the church are called the bride of Jesus. The concept is that we are like an engaged bride waiting to be joined to our heavenly Bridegroom. In the meantime we are to be faithful to Him. We are not to be pursuing other lovers. We are to be consecrated and set apart totally for Him. One day Jesus Christ, our heavenly Bridegroom, is going to return, and we are going to be joined with Him for the great wedding feast of the Lamb.

I have a question to ask you at this point: Are you a member of the bride of Christ? Are you a follower of Jesus? Do you know Him in a personal way? God has demonstrated His love toward you in that while you were yet a sinner, Christ died for you.

We talked earlier about God's perfect love. This love was never demonstrated more clearly than when Jesus came and died on the cross. It is declared in Scripture that "God so loved *[agape]* the world that He gave His only begotten Son, that whosoever believeth in Him should not perish but have everlasting life."[2]

If you do not know Jesus Christ in a personal way, let Him come and be the Lord of your life. Let Him come and be the One who will fill the loneliness deep inside your heart. And let Him give you the hope of eternal life. Not only is that the starting point for a successful marriage, but it is the foundation for all of life.

1. Matthew 7:24-27.
2. John 3:16.

Greg Laurie is the pastor of Harvest Christian Fellowship, a growing church in Southern California where thousands of people attend each week.

For more than ten years Greg has been counseling men and women of all ages. He has written several books and speaks extensively on the subject of personal relationships. He is also heard coast-to-coast on his daily radio broadcast.

He is dedicated to bringing the Word of God in a fresh, contemporary style to a generation facing the pressures and challenges of our changing world.

Greg wants to share with you **God's Design for Christian Dating,** a topic of vital importance to more than 19 million singles in our country.